# BURNI[NG] DOWN SOUTH

## Cherished Low Country Flavors
## Created in an Iconic Hotspot

### Chef David Vincent Young

*To my good friends Donna and Jim, these recipes are just for you written with Love!!*

*Your chef always*

*Dvy*

*4-8-10*

Outskirts Press, Inc.
Denver, Colorado

MW01056446

BURNIN' DOWN SOUTH
Cherished Low Country Flavors Created in an Iconic Hotspot
All Rights Reserved.
Copyright © 2008 Chef David Vincent Young
v3.0

Outskirts Press, Inc.
http://www.outskirtspress.com

ISBN: 978-1-4327-2464-1

Outskirts Press and the "OP" logo are trademarks belonging to Outskirts Press, Inc.

PRINTED IN THE UNITED STATES OF AMERICA

# Table of Contents

# Welcome
# To
# BURNIN' DOWN SOUTH
# Cherished Low Country Flavors
# Created In an Iconic Hotspot

THANK YOU FOR ALL OF YOUR LOVE, PRAYERS AND SUPPORT!

This cookbook is dedicated to Janet and my kids, my family
and ancestors, my friends, the locals and all of my customers.
All of my recipes were created with love, with hope
you will share in the fun of cooking.

BURNIN' DOWN SOUTH is an eclectic collection of
Low Country Recipes I created as a Native Hilton Head Islander
Chef David Vincent Young

Specializing in fine Low Country Cuisine, such as, Red Rice, Collards,
Shrimp Gumbo, Stewed tomato and okra, Sweet Potato Cornbread and more.

# *Foreword*
# *By*
# *Sue Ade*

When a successful chef writes a cookbook, it's something like receiving a love letter in which the author expresses a passion for cooking and exposes those coveted secrets called recipes. Native Hilton Head Islander, David Young, who descends from a family who has lived on this South Carolina barrier island since the 1700s, has written an inspired cookbook that is rich with Southern charm and local flavor with offerings like Shrimp Gumbo, Collard Greens, Red Rice and Sweet Potato Cornbread. But, David reveals a sweeter side, too, with dessert recipes that will leave you swooning. His recipe for Sweet Potato Cheese Cake pie, in which hot mashed sweet potatoes are mixed with ingredients like cream cheese, brown sugar, fragrant spices, brandy and sweet potato syrup, is so addictively delicious, so luscious, that I'd gladly purchase the *Burnin' Down South* cookbook for that one recipe alone. Understanding the ability of food to nourish the body, as well as the spirit, and remembering the many special relationships that had influence on his laid back and unique way of cooking, Young wears his sizeable heart on every page of this much anticipated cookbook. As you leaf through *Burnin' Down South*, make yourself comfortable, grab a tall glass of sweet tea and be prepared to linger awhile as you decide which of David's recipe's to try first. If you can't decide, start with the Sweet Potato Cheese Cake pie. You'll be glad you did.

Sue Ade, Syndicated Food Writer, Morris News Service
Food columnist - Hilton Head Today, Bluffton Today and Hardeeville Today

# DCHEF'S HERBS and SPICES

*To substitute dry herbs for fresh, use 1/3 teaspoon powdered or 1 teaspoon crushed for every tablespoon of chopped fresh herbs.*

## Herbs of Provence
This mixture typically contains basil, fennel seed, lavender, marjoram, rosemary, sage, savory and thyme. This is a classic blend from the South of France. Most commonly used to season fish, meats, gumbo and stews. I use these herbs in rice and all of my vegetable dishes, soups and stews.

## Thyme
Leaves of thyme are very tiny and may be used with any meat or vegetable. I add thyme to all my vegetable dishes, gumbo, chowders and bisques.

## Oregano
Small oval leaves that are used in a variety of sauces, also used with poultry, beef, lamb and vegetables. They are known for their pungent aroma. Oregano is especially popular in tomato dishes.

## Basil
Known as "The Royal Herb" these leaves are versatile. They have great affinity for tomatoes, fish and egg dishes; they are also good in almost all savory dishes.

## Rosemary
Leaves are shaped like pine needles with an extremely pungent pine aroma and flavor. Best used chopped in marinades and as a flavoring for roasted meats.

## Parsley
These plants in their entirety (root, leaves, and stems) have a high vitamin A content. They are very flavorful in themselves. They are used to blend flavors of other herbs. They also have the power to eliminate the scent of onions and garlic. They can be used in any salad, meat or soup. The stems are used in stocks for their strength of flavor and in that they do not discolor the stock. They are commonly used as a garnish to flavor, soups, sauces, dressings and other dishes.

## Ginger

Ginger rhizomes (roots) are juicy and fleshy and have a mild taste. Powdered dry ginger root is most commonly known to give spiciness to ginger snaps, gingerbread and other recipes. Ground and fresh ginger taste quite different. Ground ginger is not a good substitute for fresh ginger. Fresh ginger can be substituted for ground ginger. The ratio is 6 parts fresh to 1 part ground.

## Cinnamon

True cinnamon, is the bark of a tree that grows in Sri Lanka. It is very mild whether rolled into a tight quill or stick or in powdered form. It is used in many desserts.

## Nutmeg

Has a slightly sweet flavor. It is used primarily in desserts

## Garlic

Garlic is usually cooked with other foods to give flavor to soups, sauces, pasta dishes and stews. Raw garlic is very powerful, when it is cooked its flavor melds in with the other ingredients, but you still can taste it in the background. It is a very delicious addition to food.

## Restaurant grind black pepper

This is made from coarsely ground black peppercorns. They have a more robust and spicy flavor and texture.

## *Jamaican jerk seasoning*

This is a fiery spice rub native to Jamaica. The two main ingredients are allspice and scotch bonnet peppers. Other ingredients include cloves, cinnamon, scallions, nutmeg, thyme and garlic. These spices are mixed together to make a marinade used on meats and fish.

# EVERYTHING SWEET POTATO

## History of the Sweet Potato

### *THE SWEET POTATO AND THE YAM: ALIKE OR DIFFERENT?*

The sweet potato is native to the Western hemisphere. It is widely enjoyed in North, Central and South America because of its versatility in breads, desserts and as a vegetable. There are many varieties of the sweet potato, but the two most widely available are the yellow sweet potato and the bright-orange sweet potato. The orange, sweet potatoes are erroneously called yams. The true yam comes from Africa and was introduced to the Americas via the slave trade. It is a brownish tuber with a coarse, almost "hairy" skin and off-white to yellow flesh-not at all like our sweet potato in appearance.

Although quite similar, sweet potatoes and true yams are from very different plant families. Yam is an English derivative of the African word "nyami" referring to the starchy, edible root of the Dioscorea plants. Sweet potatoes have white flesh. When producers and shippers initiated production of the orange-fleshed sweet potato into the southern United States, producers and shippers needed to distinguish them from the white-fleshed type. Most yams marketed in the United States actually are sweet potatoes with a relatively moist texture and orange flesh. Although "sweet potato" and "yam" are generally used interchangeably, the U.S. Department of Agriculture requires that sweet potatoes be distributed under the label "yam" and always be accompanied by the label "sweet potato" to differentiate them from true yams. Unprocessed sweet potatoes do not have an extremely long shelf life compared to other vegetables like turnips, carrots or potatoes.

In the South, or for my purposes, the Low Country, sweet potatoes are a local (and regional) favorite, whether served with fresh fish, baked and eaten with vanilla ice cream, or used in soup, corn bread, or pie.

Native Americans were already growing sweet potatoes when Columbus and his shipmates arrived in 1492. In the South, sweet potatoes were cultivated and frequently used by African slaves. They used this vegetable interchangeably with the yam, which is indigenous to Africa and some Latin American countries.

The yam and sweet potato are still used interchangeably today, even though they come from two different plants. The two tubers are similar in size and shape. Yams contain a higher moisture and sugar content than sweet potatoes. Sweet potatoes are grown in this country, and yams are not. Sweet potatoes are often called yams in recipes. Canned sweet potatoes are usually labeled as yams or candied yams. If a recipe calls for sweet potatoes or yams, you can use either one and come out with the same end result.

# Nutritional Information
## The Sweet Potato Is a Good Source of Nutrition

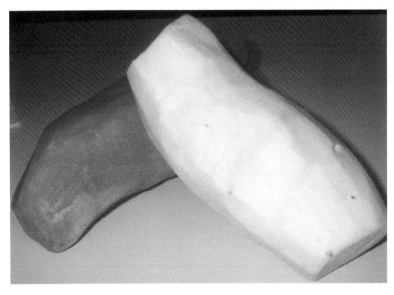

There are two main types of sweet potatoes. The one most commonly called a sweet potato has flesh that is relatively dry and fluffy, with a yellow color and starchy texture. Yams are moister, sweeter, and more slender and have skins that range from orange to purple.

The flesh of the sweet potato ranges in color from white to orange. The nutritional value varies between varieties.

The orange-fleshed potatoes are very rich in beta carotene.

White-fleshed varieties are a good source of vitamin C but the orange-fleshed sweet potatoes are much richer in vitamin C. Orange-fleshed sweet potatoes have more sugar, mostly sucrose, and dietary fiber, while the white-fleshed sweet potatoes are higher in starch.

The sweet potato is also a good source of vitamin E and sweet potatoes are a naturally fat-free food.

The sweet potato is a nutritious and economical food. It is low in sodium and a good source of fiber and other important vitamins and minerals. They are a complex carbohydrate food source.

When shopping for sweet potatoes, select firm, well-shaped potatoes with smooth skin. Avoid those with soft spots, bruises or any signs of decay. Also remember what you are buying them for. Once you get your sweet potatoes home, make sure not to refrigerate them unless they are cooked. Cold temperatures can cause them to become bitter. Instead, store them in a cool, dry place and use them within a week or two. When cutting a sweet potato always use a stainless steel knife and place them into cold water to prevent darkening.

Sweet potatoes are a vegetable. The recommended daily allowance of vegetables is two to four servings daily. Sweet potatoes are low in sodium, cholesterol free, fat free, high in fiber, contain minerals and vitamins A, C and E. Sweet potatoes are also more nutritious if cooked with the skin on. They are also rich in beta-carotene (a special kind of vitamin A). This vitamin helps your body wage war against free-radicals. Free-radicals try to damage your cells, but beta-carotene coats your cells and helps your immune system fight back. Sweet potatoes are good for your health!

Sweet Potatoes compliment almost all meats and fish. They are great in stews, soups, and salads or baked in breads, pies, custards and cakes. They naturally go well with other sweet vegetables such as beets, parsnips and carrots. Sweet potatoes are very delicious simply baked in their skins or steamed. They are probably most recognized in their traditional holiday forms as candied yams or in pies. They are great pureed and can be used in savory or sweet foods.

Scrub sweet potatoes well before you cook them. Organically grown sweet potatoes are the best, if you want to eat the skins. Remove the ends, then slice, dice, shred or bake them whole. Once they are peeled or sliced, it is best to hold them in water to prevent oxidizing if they are not going to be cooked for some time. Sweet potatoes do not have the same starch content as regular potatoes, Therefore so it is not recommended to interchange them in a recipe calling for white potatoes unless you use some of both.

Sweet potatoes vary in weight from about four ounces to about one pound. One pound of sweet potatoes (three medium potatoes) yields three to four cups raw sliced, or diced, two and one half cups cooked or about one and three quarters cups mashed. A single serving of sweet potato is four ounces.

The Sweet Potato goes well with roasts, especially when blended with Yukon gold and purple potatoes.

## NUTRITIONAL ANALYSIS
### Sweet Potato
#### 4oz serving size

|  | Baked in skin | Boiled in skin | Candied |
|---|---|---|---|
| Calories | 141 | 114 | 168 |
| Protein (g) | 2.1 | 1.7 | 1.3 |
| Fat (g) | .5 | .4 | 3.3 |
| Carbohydrates (g) | 32.5 | 26.3 | 34.2 |
| Calcium | 40 | 32 | 37 |
| Iron | .9 | .7 | .9 |
| Sodium | 12 | 10 | 42 |
| Potassium | 300 | 243 | 190 |
| Vitamin A (mg) | 8,100 | 7,900 | 6,300 |
| Thiamine | .09 | .09 | .06 |
| Riboflavin | .07 | .06 | .04 |
| Niacin | .7 | .6 | .4 |

# Sweet Potato Cornbread

*It took over a year to perfect this recipe. It is easier for me to make something just from feeling and tasting, rather than harnessing a flavor with words and writing them down, I had to test many different formulations and ingredients to find the perfect union of flavor and spice. After many taste tests, here it is. I wrote it just for you.*

# Dchefs' Sweet Potato Cornbread™

*I did not want to give you the same old cornbread, I was not satisfied with basic cornbread, and I hated it because the flavor did not punch me in the taste buds. I wanted to make something that was unique, so I took two traditional ingredients, corn meal and sweet potatoes and created a new taste sensation.*

*Makes two 12x13x2 square baking pans servings depends on how the bread is cut*

### Part1: Infuse the sweet potato with simple syrup
This recipe starts with cooking the sweet potatoes in simple syrup. This is also the beginning process for making candied yams (sweet potatoes). The process of cooking the sweet potatoes in the simple syrup really intensifies the flavor of the sweet potato.

**Step1: Boil the sweet potato and make sweet potato syrup.**
1. Scrub and peel 6 medium sweet potatoes.
2. Cut potatoes into medium diced pieces. Place in a 4 quart sauce pan.
3. Add 3 cups of sugar and 1 cup of light brown sugar packed. Cover potatoes with water.
4. Boil until tender, 25 to 35 minutes. Test for doneness with a fork
5. Drain, and reserve the sweet potato simple syrup. Bring the simple syrup back to a boil. Boil until syrup thickens. Allow to cool. Reserve the syrup for other uses. This syrup is used as a glaze to top the sweet potato cornbread when comes out of the oven.
6. Hold the sweet potatoes in a large bowl or baking pan.
*Note: Use in the sweet potato cornbread, bread pudding and other recipes in the book that call for boiled sweet potatoes.*

**Step2: Sweet potato cornbread batter**
*Ingredients*
2 cups fine cornmeal
2 cups medium to coarse cornmeal

2 cups all-purpose flour
1 cup white granulated sugar
½ pound light brown sugar
6 tablespoons baking powder
¼ cup ground ginger
1 to 2 tablespoon Jamaican Jerk seasoning
1 ½ tablespoons cinnamon
2 cups sour dressing (imitation sour cream) or sour cream
1 cup liquid margarine or melted butter flavored shortening
4oz cup vanilla extract
3 to 4 cups Water (use as needed) if the mixture is too dry use more water.
6 cups boiled sweet potatoes from **step1** above. (Do not pack in cup)

### *Method*
1. In a large mixing bowl, combine all dry ingredients, mix well to incorporate (disperse) all ingredients.
2. Make a well in the center of mixture.
3. Add vanilla, shortening, sour cream and 2 cups of sweet potatoes.
4. Mix with a rubber spatula from the center. Add 1 cup of water at a time. Mix well. The batter should be soft but not runny.
5. Fold in remaining sweet potatoes.
6. Moderately grease baking pans. Fill each pan about ¾ full.
7. Bake in a 350º oven for 60 to 90 min. check for doneness by inserting a knife or toothpick. When inserted and comes out clean, cornbread is done.
8. Remove from oven and drizzle with sweet potato syrup. Cool for 30 minutes then serve.

# Sweet Potato Bread Pudding

*Makes 2 9x13 baking pans*
### Ingredients
1 cup Butter
1 ½ quarts Heavy Cream
2 cans Sweetened Condensed Milk
Zest from two lemons finely diced
2 Teaspoons fresh lemon juice
1 Tablespoon vanilla extract
½ cup light brown sugar
1 Tablespoon ground ginger
2 teaspoons cinnamon
3 ½ quarts Toasted bread crumbs
6 eggs
5 to 6 cups boiled sweet potatoes (not packed) for preparation see sweet potato cornbread recipe.
### Method
1. Crumble bread place on a baking sheet and toast until golden in color.
2. In a 4 quart sauce pan, add butter and Heavy Cream. Put on medium heat to melt butter stirring constantly. Do not boil. When the Butter has melted, add sweet milk, sugar, lemon zest, vanilla and spices.
3. Slowly stir in bread crumbs. Mix well. Stir in eggs and lemon juice. Mix all together well.
4. Grease baking pans, to each pan spread out 2 to 3 cups of the boiled sweet potatoes. Spoon bread pudding mixture over the potatoes. Bake at 350° for 30 minutes.  Serve warm. Top with lemon curd or sweet potato syrup.

## Steamed Sweet Potatoes

Scrub sweet potatoes. They can be left whole or cut them into large pieces. Steam covered or in boiling water until tender when pierced with a fork. Cooking time is 30 to 40 minutes depending on the size of the potato.

## Grilled Sweet Potatoes

Use steamed or boiled potatoes. Cut them into desired shapes or just in half. Brush with vegetable oil and season as you desire. Cajun spice or jerk spice work well or just salt, pepper, garlic and herbs will do. Place potatoes on grill turning then 45 degrees after 5 minutes. Cook on one or both sides.

## Boiled Sweet Potatoes

Results with this method of cooking can vary depending on the moisture content of the sweet potato that you are using.

### Method 1
Leave unpeeled potatoes whole. Sometimes if you cut into chunks before cooking they may tend to become waterlogged. Cover potato with cold water and bring to a boil. The water can be salted. Reduce heat and simmer until fork tender. When the potatoes are done, peel and season. Serve sliced or mashed don't forget the butter.

### Method 2
Peel and dice the potatoes. Cover them with cold water. For savory add vegetable base. For use in desserts add sugar as if you were making a simple syrup. Bring to a boil then simmer gently until tender. Remove potatoes. The savory broth can be used in soups or bread. The simple syrup can be reduced to make sweet potato syrup.

# Sunrise Potatoes

*These will wake up your taste buds. I made these in the morning the*
*color arrangement made me think of the sun. Good morning!*
*Make these with eggs and bacon*
*When these potatoes were arranged on the grill in a circle with*
*sweet potatoes around the perimeter it looks like the sun*

### Ingredients
2 Large Yukon Gold Potatoes
1 medium to jumbo Sweet Potato
½ cup onions, medium dice
¼ cup diced, green bell peppers
¼ cup diced, red bell peppers
3 tbsp unsalted
**To season: use sparingly**, 1 tsp restaurant grind black pepper, 1 tsp granulated garlic, 1 tsp Herbs of Provence, 2 tsp dry parsley and salt to taste.

### Method
1. Peel and cube potatoes. Keep separate.
2. Place potatoes in 2 separate 3 quart sauce pans.
3. For the Yukon Gold, Lightly season water with salt, Boil 25 minutes until fork tender drain well and reserve. For Sweet potato, lightly sweeten the water and then add 2 tsp salt. Boil 25 minutes until fork tender. Drain and reserve.
4. Heat a large skillet or grill to 325º. Melt butter; add onions and peppers, sauté till onion are translucent. Add Yukon potatoes then add sweet potatoes. **Season sparingly.** Cook until potatoes are hot and onions are golden brown. Serve Hot!

# Simple Syrup

*Makes 4 cups*

Simple Syrup is a simple mixture of 2 parts sugar and 1 part water. When infused with, for our purposes, sweet potatoes, or blue berries, it adds not only sweetness but intensifies flavor as well.

## Ingredients
4 cups sugar
2 cups water

## Method
1. Combine in 4 quart sauce pan
2. Cook over low heat, stirring occasionally, until sugar is dissolved.
3. Simmer covered, for 5 minutes. Allow to cool. Chill until needed.
4. Store syrup in a glass, or plastic container. Simple syrup can be stored in refrigeration for up to 6 months.

# Baked Sweet Potatoes
*Can be eaten as a side or mashed to be used in desserts*

*Makes 4 to 6 servings*

## Ingredients
4 to 6 sweet potatoes, scrubbed
1 tablespoon vegetable, corn, or olive oil

## Method
1. Preheat oven to 350°.
2. Rub the sweet potatoes with the oil.
3. Place them on a baking sheet and bake for 45 to 60 minutes or until they give when lightly squeezed.
4. Serve hot out of the oven, with butter, mash or cool for use in another recipe.

# *Mashed Sweet Potatoes*
## *Most commonly used as a side dish*

*Serves 5*

### *Ingredients*
4 medium sized sweet potatoes
Salt to taste
Black pepper to taste
4 tablespoons butter
If you desire add a pinch of garlic and Herbs of Provence

### *Method*
Peel and cut potatoes into quarters. Place into a 4 quart sauce pan and cover with water. Add 2 teaspoons salt. Bring to a boil and cook until tender 30 to 40 minutes. When the potatoes are fork tender, drain water and add potatoes to a medium sized bowl. Add butter and black pepper. Whip potatoes until smooth. Season to taste with salt and pepper. Serve hot.

# Mashed Sweet & Yukon Gold Potatoes
# With Roasted Garlic

*Serves 12 to 15*
*Add Yukon Gold Potato to Mashed Sweet Potato, butter, garlic, salt, pepper and cream for an excellent garlic mashed potato.*

## Ingredients
6 medium Yukon gold potatoes peel and cut into halves or fourths.
4 medium sweet potatoes peeled and cut into fourths.
Approximately- 8 to 16 oz Heavy Cream
1/8 cup roasted garlic
¼ to ½ cup of Butter
Salt and pepper to taste
1 cup shredded parmesan cheese. Optional- this adds a tasty finishing touch.

**To make Roasted garlic** use: 2 heads of garlic. Separate into cloves and peel.
1 cup vegetable oil. Pre-heat oven to 350º
Place garlic and oil into a small ovenproof baking dish. Cover and bake for 20 to 30 minutes until the garlic is soft and starts to look golden brown. The flavor of garlic becomes rich, sweet and smoky after roasting. Remove from oven and allow the mixture to cool. Remove garlic from oil and chop to a fine consistency return to oil and use as needed. Garlic oil can be stored in an air tight container and refrigerated for up to four weeks.

## Method
1. Place all potatoes in to a 4 quart heavy sauce pan.
2. Cover with water and add 1 tablespoon of salt.
3. Bring to a boil and cook until tender. 20 to 30 minutes.
4. Drain and add to a medium mixing bowl. Add all other ingredients except cream. Mix well. Add cream 1 cup at a time. Mix well. If to thick add more cream as needed.
5. Season to taste with salt and pepper.
*Optional add shredded parmesan cheese. Mix well and serve.*

# Candied Sweet Potatoes

Step1
1. Scrub and peel 3 medium sweet potatoes.
2. Cut potatoes into medium diced pieces.
3. Cover with water and 2 cups of sugar.
4. Boil until tender. 12-14 minutes.
5. Drain, and reserve the sweet potato simple syrup. Bring the simple syrup back to a boil. Boil until syrup thickens.
6. Place the sweet potatoes in a baking pan. **(Use in desserts that call for mashed sweet potatoes)**
Step2
1. Sprinkle in 1 teaspoon vanilla, cinnamon and ginger.
2. Top with a ¼ cup butter and ½ cup brown sugar and pecan pieces.
3. Bake at 350° until sugar caramelizes. Drizzle with 1 cup of sweet potato syrup.
4. Serve warm with whipped cream.
This recipe features the sweet potato syrup used to top the Sweet Potato Cornbread.

# Sweet Potato Scones

*Makes 12 scones*

### Ingredients
4 tablespoons Butter
¼ cup light brown sugar packed
1 large egg
2 tablespoons golden syrup or sweet potato syrup
1 cup mashed sweet potatoes
3 ½ cups + 1 tablespoon sifted self-rising flour
1 teaspoon cinnamon
1 teaspoon ginger
1/3 cup milk

*Method:* Pre-heat oven to 350°
1. Cream 4 tbsp butter with ¼ cup castor sugar until combined.
2. Gradually beat in 1 egg and 2 tablespoons golden syrup.
3. Stir in 1 cup mashed sweet potato, 3½ cups + 1tbsp sifted self-raising flour, 1 teaspoon cinnamon and 1/3 cup milk.
4. Knead on a lightly floured surface and pat dough out until ½ inch thick.
5. Cut into 12 rounds. Place in well-greased 9 inch round cake or baking pan, brush tops with half & half creamer then bake in a 350° oven for 20 minutes.

# *Sweet Potato Cheese Cake Pie*

Makes 1 10 inch deep dish pie

## *Ingredients*
16 oz cream cheese at room temp
1 to 2 cups hot mashed sweet potatoes (use sweet potato cornbread recipe for potato)
½ cup sweetened condensed milk
½ cup light brown sugar packed
3 large room temperate eggs
½ teaspoon Cinnamon   ½ teaspoon Ginger
¼ teaspoon nutmeg
1 ½ teaspoons vanilla
¼ cup of E&J Brandy
2 tablespoons flour
2 tablespoons Sweet Potato syrup or molasses

## *Method*
1. Pre heat oven to 350º.
2. In a large mixing bowl combine sugar, spices, condensed milk, and cream cheese. Beat ingredients together until smooth. Mix in Sweet potatoes and the remaining ingredients, flour, eggs, molasses, vanilla, and the Brandy. Mix until smooth.
3. Pour batter into crust. (Store bought graham crust, or make your own)
4. Bake for 30 minutes to 45 minutes or until filling has set. When done set on a cooling rack to bring temperature to room temp. Serve chilled with whipped cream and sweet potato syrup.


# *Graham Cracker or Ginger Snap pie crust*

3 cups graham cracker or Ginger Snap crumbs
8 tablespoons unsalted melted butter
*Method:* In a medium sized bowl combine crumbs and butter. Mix. Press into pie pan. Use as needed

# *Dchefs' Sweet Potato Bread*

1 9x5x3 Loaf pan greased and floured
Oven temp 350°                     Bake time: 1 hour 15 minutes

## *Ingredients*
5 Tablespoons unsalted butter, room temp
½ cup sugar
½ cup light brown sugar packed
1 large egg
2 egg whites
1 teaspoon vanilla extract
1 teaspoon baking soda
½ teaspoon salt
¼ teaspoon baking powder
1 ¾ cups all-purpose flour
1 ½ cup mashed sweet potatoes
½ cup of heavy cream or vanilla yogurt
1/3 cup chopped pecans

## *Method*
1. Cream together, butter and sugar until light and fluffy. Add egg and mix well. Add egg whites and vanilla. Beat well
2. Add mashed sweet potatoes. Beat on high for 30 seconds.
3. Combine all dry ingredients except the nuts. Sift 3 times. Add in flour and cream or yogurt alternating. Mix well after each addition. Add nuts mix well. Pour into pan. Bake 1 hour 15 minutes until brown. Test for doneness with a toothpick. When the tooth pick is inserted and comes out clean, Bread is done.

# Sweet Potato Soufflé

*Serves 12*

## Ingredients
**Sweet Potato mixture**
4 cups cooked and mashed sweet potatoes
¾ cup white sugar
¼ teaspoon ginger
¼ teaspoon cinnamon
¼ teaspoon nutmeg
1/3 cup plus 2 tablespoons butter, room temp
3 eggs
1 teaspoon vanilla extract
½ cup heavy cream

## Method
1. Combine the mashed sweet potatoes with the white sugar, butter, beaten eggs, vanilla, spices and heavy cream.
2. Spread mixture into a 2 quart oven-safe baking dish.

Step 2
**Coconut Oat Topping**
1 cup flaked coconut
1/3 cup all purpose flour
¼ cup rolled oats
¼ teaspoon ginger
¼ teaspoon cinnamon
1 cup packed brown sugar
1 cup pecan pieces
1/3 cup melted butter

1. Combine all ingredients, and sprinkle over top of potatoes.
2. Bake at 350° for 30 to 35 minutes.

# *Sweet Potato Cake with Chocolate chip swirl*

Use a bundt cake pan greased and floured
Oven temp 350º            Bake time 60 to 70 minutes

## *Ingredients*
Part1
2 pounds Sweet potatoes mashed
4 large eggs
1 teaspoon vanilla
1 cup vegetable oil
1 cup mini chocolate chips
Mix these ingredients in a large bowl.

## *Ingredients*
3 cups all-purpose flour
1 ½ cups granulated sugar
1 teaspoon salt
2 teaspoon baking powder
2 teaspoon baking soda
2 teaspoons cinnamon
1 teaspoon nutmeg
 ½ teaspoon ginger
¼ teaspoon cloves
Combine and sift these dry ingredients into a large bowl. Combine with the potato mixture.
Mix in 1 cup chopped nuts.

## For the swirl
1. Take 1/3 of the batter and mix with 4 oz of melted chocolate.
2. Spoon Batter into pan, alternating the chocolate batter with the plain batter. Cut together with a knife or wooden spoon handle to marble the mixture. Bake for 60 to 70 min. done, when toothpick inserted comes out clean

# NATIVE TREATS

## Low Country Fruit Cobbler

9x13 baking pan or casserole baking dish buttered or greased
Pre-heat oven to 350º
This recipe started out as Peach cobbler, one of my favorite flavors. I have added a little twist and a couple tasty options.

## Cobbler Batter

### Ingredients

1 cup Bisquick Baking Mix          1 cup evaporated milk or yogurt
½ teaspoon cinnamon                ½ teaspoon nutmeg
¼ teaspoon ground ginger           ½ cup sugar
1 large egg                        ½ cup unsalted softened

This batter works very well with the cobbler.
In a large mixing bowl.
1. Mix flour with other dry ingredients. Add milk or yogurt. Mix well
2. Mix in butter. Spoon batter into a well greased baking dish with the **cobbler filling**.
3. Sprinkle the batter and cobbler filling with crunchy oat topping.
4. Bake 50 to 60 minutes. At 350º

## Cobbler Filling

### Ingredients

3 mangoes peeled and diced
1 can (29oz) sliced peaches drain.
½ cup sugar
¼ teaspoon ginger
¼ teaspoon cinnamon
1 tablespoon corn starch or flour
*twist* add 1 cup 1 inch cubed cooked sweet potatoes to the filling.
Combine all ingredients in a large mixing bowl. Use as needed.

# Crunchy Oat Topping

**Ingredients**

2 cups Rolled Oats                    ¼ cup all-purpose flour
½ teaspoon salt                       ½ teaspoon cinnamon
½ cup chopped nuts                    3 tablespoons brown sugar
6 tablespoons melted unsalted butter

Mix ingredients use as topping or streusel.

*twist- add a ½ cup coconut flakes. This addition will yum it up some!

*Option*

Another tasty option would be to use a pastry crust. This can be used for the top and bottom

# Pastry Crust

This is your basic pastry crust. This can be used in savory dishes as well as desserts.

3 cups all-purpose flour
2 tablespoons granulated sugar
2 teaspoons baking powder
1 teaspoon salt
½ cup (1 stick) unsalted butter
½ cup solid vegetable shortening
10 tablespoons cold water

*Method*

1. Combine and sift all dry ingredients in a large bowl.
2. Cut the butter into ½ inch cubes and disperse them over the sifted flour mixture. Do the same with the shortening
3. With 2 knives using a scissor motion or a pastry blender, cut in the butter and shortening at little at a time until the mixture resembles cornmeal.
4. Sprinkle the water over the flour mixture. Blend with fingers until combined.
5. Divide mixture in ½ and shape into disks. Refrigerate to cool and rest until you are ready to use it.
6. On a lightly floured surface, use a rolling pin dusted with flour; roll out one of the pastry disks to 12 inches in diameter.

**For use in cobbler**

Transfer pastry disk to greased 9 inch baking pan. Add cobbler filling. Roll out other disk to top cobbler. Pick edges of top and bottom pastry crusts together to seal.

## Egg wash and sugar topping

1 large egg
1 teaspoon ½ and ½
3 tablespoons granulated sugar
For topping, whisk together ½ and ½ with egg until combined.
Use a pastry brush to apply egg wash. Sprinkle sugar over pastry.
Use the point of a sharp knife to cut several slits through the top of the pastry.
Bake at 350º for 30 to 45 minutes, or until the pastry is golden brown and the filling is bubbling.
Serve warm or at room temp.

## About self-Rising flour

**Self-rising flour that is store bought is a** white four to which baking powder has been added (sometimes salt in addition). Its advantage is that the baking powder is blended in very evenly. Usage is limited by two facts: 1ˢᵗ, different formulas call for different proportions of baking powder. No single blend is right for all purposes. 2ⁿᵈ baking powder loses its leavening power over time. Quality of baked goods made from this four can fluctuate.

## Home-made self rising flour

Most often used for quick breads, biscuits, and pancakes.
1 ½ teaspoon baking powder and a ½ teaspoon salt per cup of all-purpose flour. The salt can be omitted.

### METHOD
To make 2 cups: Use 2 cups all-purpose flour and 3 teaspoons baking powder (salt 1 teaspoon)
To make 4 cups: Use 4 cups all-purpose flour and 6 teaspoons baking powder (salt 2 teaspoons)
To make 6 cups: Use 6 cups all-purpose flour and 9 teaspoon baking powder (salt 3 teaspoons)
**Sift 3 times**. Now use flour as needed in your recipes.
HAPPY BAKING!
**Store the flour, in an air tight container with a tight fitting lid**.

# *Quick Biscuits*

## *Ingredients*
2 ¼ cups self-rising flour
¼ cup butter flavored Crisco
1 ½ tablespoons sugar
¼ teaspoon salt
1 cup milk

## *Method*
1. Combine and mix all dry ingredients together thoroughly in a medium bowl.
2. Cut shortening into flour mixture. Stir until mixture looks mealy
3. Add milk and mix together.
4. Pour mixture out on a floured surface. Knead a few times dusting with flour if the mix is too sticky. Double fold then pat or roll out to about ½ inch thick. Cut biscuits with a biscuit cutter. Be sure to flour the blade
5. Bake on a cookie sheet at 400º, for 20-25 minutes

# Blonde Pecan Pie

*This is a confectionary delight; this pie is unlike the traditional pecan pie both in flavor and texture.*

### Makes 2 10 inch pies

Step1: In a large mixing Bowl
### Ingredients
4 cans sweetened condensed milk
12 large whole eggs
½ cup Brandy E&J
2 tablespoons vanilla
¼ teaspoon nutmeg
¾ teaspoon cinnamon
1 ½ teaspoon ground ginger
1 ½ cups packed light brown sugar
2 10 inch graham cracker pie shells
4 cups pecan pieces

### Method
1. Combine all ingredients and mix well.
2. In each pie shell pour 2 cups of pecans.
3. Pour blonde pecan batter over pecans.
4. Place pies on sheet pan. Bake at 325° for 45 minutes

# Classic Pecan Pie

*Makes one 9 inch pie*

## Ingredients
1 unbaked pie shell or 1 graham cracker pie shell or use pastry crust
¼ cup Butter
1 cup Sugar
2 teaspoon Vanilla extract
1 teaspoon fresh lemon juice
1 teaspoon ground ginger
¼ teaspoon cinnamon
4 eggs beaten
¾ cup dark sugar cane syrup
1 ½ cups Pecans

## Method
1. Cream together, butter, sugar, vanilla, lemon juice, ginger and cinnamon.
2. Beat in eggs and syrup.
3. Stir in pecans.
4. Pour into pie shell
5. Put into a pre-heated 350º oven. Bake 30 to 40 minutes or until done when a knife inserted comes out clean.
Be careful not to burn!

# Pecan Golf balls

## Ingredients

2 cups all-purpose flour
2 cups finely chopped pecans
½ cup brown sugar
1 cup of softened unsalted butter
½ tsp ground ginger
1 tsp vanilla
3 cups 10x powdered sugar for rolling Golf Balls

## Method

1. Preheat oven to 325º.
2. In a large mixing bowl, Combine, Brown Sugar, butter and vanilla.
3. Cream at medium speed until well blended.
4. Combine flour and ginger, sift to incorporate.
5. Add flour and pecans to the butter mixture. Mix on low speed, scrape bowl often, until mixed well. Mix approx 3 to 4 min.
6. Shape dough into 1 inch balls.
7. Place dough balls on an ungreased cookie sheet.
Bake cookies for 18 to 25 minutes, or until very lightly browned.
8. Remove from oven immediately. Allow Golf balls to sit for a couple minutes to cool then **Roll** in powdered sugar while still warm and once more when they are cooled. Store in tins or serve to your family and best friends.
I like them with egg nog.

# *Blueberry Key-Lime Pie*

*Makes 2 10 inch pies*
*Step1: Cook Blue Berries*

### Ingredients
1 ½ cups frozen blue berries
1 cup water
2 cups sugar

### Method
1. Dissolve sugar into water and bring to a boil.
2. Add blue berries. Boil until liquid thickens.
3. Strain blueberries and reserve the syrup.

*Step 2*
Key-Lime Mixture
### Ingredients
4 cans sweetened condensed milk
4 whole large eggs
12 egg yolks
1 cup Nelly and Joe's Key-lime Juice

### Method
1. Combine all ingredients and mix well.
2. Fill two 10 inch graham cracker pie shells ½ full.
3. Sprinkle layer with the cooked blue berries.
4. Cover blue berries with key-lime batter to with in ¼ inch of pie rim.
5. Drizzle pie with blue berry sauce. Use a toothpick to swirl top of pie.
6. Lightly sprinkle top of pie with blue berries.
7. Bake at 325° for about 45 minutes.
Remove pie from oven. Allow it to cool to room temp and then putting it into the refrigerator.
This pie must be given time to set in order for it to cut well.
I like to make this one a day ahead of time.
Serve with whipped cream and the reserved blue berries with sauce.

# Key-Lime Pie

Makes 2 10 inch pies

Key-Lime Mixture
**Ingredients**
4 cans sweetened condensed milk
4 whole large eggs
12 egg yolks 1 cup
1 cup Nelly and Joe's Key-lime Juice

*Method*
1. Combine all ingredients and mix well.
2. Fill two 10 inch graham cracker pie shells 3/4 full
3. Bake at 325° for about 25 to 30 minutes.
Remove pie from oven. Allow it to cool to room temperature, and then refrigerate.

*Note: This pie must be given time to set in order for it to cut well.*
*I like to make this one a day ahead of time. Serve with a dollop of whipped cream and garnish with lime.*

# *Separating Eggs*

*NOTE*   To separate eggs have 4 containers ready. One is used to catch the whites, **2nd** used to receive yolk, **3rd** to hold clean egg whites. **4th** used to hold whites contaminated with yolk. Cold eggs separate best because the whites hold together better.

## *Method*
1. Crack egg over a container or bowl.
2. Transfer the egg back and forth between the halves of shell allowing whites to drop into bowl. This can also be done using clean hands, allowing whites to fall between fingers into a container.
3. Place yolk in separate container.
4. Inspect the egg white. If clean transfer to the whites container. The smallest bit of egg yolk, which contains fat, will cause the egg whites not to foam. Place the egg whites in a separate bowl for contaminated whites. These can be used for baking, omelets, quiches and other uses.

For our purposes the egg whites will be used to make meringue for Pavlova and angel food cake.

# *Making Meringues*

Adding sugar to beaten egg whites produces meringues. In addition to sugar, other ingredients may be added for flavor and texture.

**Common meringues** are made by first beating egg whites into soft foam (soft peaks). In a common meringue the ideal whipping temperature is 70°.

This can be achieved by placing your bowl over warm water or leaving out for 30 minutes. At room temperature beaten egg whites can foam 6 to 8 times its original volume.

Granulated sugar (super fine) is then slowly rained in and beaten or folded into the egg whites. The final product may be hard or soft depending on the ratio of sugar to egg whites. In recipes egg whites are usually measured in volume rather than by number. 8 egg whites equal 1 cup and 4 whole eggs equal 1 cup.

Always begin with a pristine clean copper or stainless steel bowl free of oil and clean and dry utensils, never use aluminum bowls as it will discolor the meringue.

Whipping egg whites is like blowing up a hot air balloon. While whipping or beating the proteins in the egg white lose their tight bonds and begin to unfold causing air to be trapped forming bubbles, sugar stiffens the foam. Fats will collapse the foam.

Fresher eggs make a more stable meringue but give you slightly less volume. To me stability is better than volume. Older eggs do give more volume but have more of a tendency to collapse.

### *Beating egg whites*

Place egg whites in to a large, tall bowl and set mixer to medium high speed, and beat the whites until they form soft peaks. If you add the sugar too early it will take twice as long to get your whites to foam. Once the egg whites have formed soft peaks, slowly rain in your sugar, beating constantly. (Superfine sugar works best because it dissolves faster than regular granulated sugar)

As a general rule, add a total of ¼ cup sugar for each egg white used. For softer meringues use 2 tablespoons of sugar per egg white used. If you use less than 2 tablespoons of sugar per egg white your meringue foam will shrink. Beat egg whites and sugar until it is smooth when ran between your fingers. The meringue is done when it is not runny, and when you can hold it on a spoon upside down and it stays and holds its shape.

*Meringue stabilizers*

1. Cream of tartar: Add 1/8 teaspoon of cream of tartar for each egg white used. This can be added in the beginning of the whipping process.
2. Cornstarch: For every four egg whites, stir 1 tablespoon of cornstarch into 1/3 cup of cold water. Heat this mixture until it thickens. Allow to cool. After the sugar has been added and beaten to soft peaks add the corn starch mixture 1 tablespoon at a time then beat to stiff peaks.

*Baking meringues:*
Over-baking causes meringues to be tough. Cook meringues to 160°.
Meringues will be more done if they are baked at a lower temp for a longer period of time. The ideal oven temperature is from 250° to 325°.
To serve baked meringue, cut with a knife dipped in cold water.

# Pavlova Payatt w/ strawberries, mango, and kiwi Drizzled w/ lemon curd

*Serves 12*
### Ingredients
13 large egg whites 1 ½ cups room temp 70 °F
1/4 teaspoon salt
2 1/2 cups superfine granulated sugar
1 1/2 tablespoons cornstarch
1 1/2 tablespoons distilled white vinegar
2 lb strawberries, halved, sliced or quartered if large
1/4 cup plus 1 1/2 tablespoons granulated sugar
1 lb sliced mangoes
6 kiwis sliced
2 1/2 cups chilled heavy cream
2 teaspoons vanilla
Special equipment: a kitchen aid 6 quart electric stand mixer

**Make meringues:** Preheat oven to 300°F and line 2 large baking sheets with parchment.
*Method (using a* Kitchen aid stand mixer)
1. Beat whites with salt until they hold soft peaks.
2. Slowly beat in 2 cups superfine sugar and continue beating until mixture holds stiff, glossy peaks.
3. Stir together remaining 1/2 cup superfine sugar and cornstarch. Beat into meringue, and then beat in vinegar. Draw 4 10 inch circles on the parchment paper and sprinkle w/ sugar. This helps prevent the Pavlova from sticking to paper.
4. Spoon 2 mounds of meringue, each about 1 inch high and 1 inch apart on each lined baking sheet. Divide any remaining meringue among mounds.
5. Bake in upper and lower thirds of oven, switching position of sheets halfway through baking, until crisp and a pale gold color on the outside but still soft inside, 1 1/2 to 2 hours total. If meringues are still not crisp after 2 hours, turn off oven and cool in oven 10 minutes.
6. Transfer from parchment to racks to cool. Carefully peel away parchment paper. (Meringues may stick if cooled completely on paper.)
7. Place one Pavlova disk on a serving plate
**Assemble 2 Pavlova's:** Just before serving, toss strawberries with lemon juice and 1/4 cup granulated sugar and let stand, tossing occasionally until sugar is dissolved. Beat cream with vanilla and remaining 1 1/2 tablespoons granulated sugar, then mound some whipped cream and fruit onto each. Top w/ another Pavlov a disk and repeat the process. Finally, drizzle the top of the Pavlova with lemon curd. Cut and serve! Enjoy!

# *Lemon Curd*

*Makes 5 cups*

## Ingredients
2/3 cup fresh squeezed lemon juice (4 to 6 medium-sized lemons)
Using fresh lemon juice gives you the best fresh citrus taste
Finely grated zest of 2 lemons
6 eggs
1 ½ cups Super fine granulated sugar
4 ounces unsalted butter room temp

## Method
1. In a stainless steel bowl places over a pan of simmering water, whisk together the eggs, sugar, lemon juice and zest.
2. Cook the mixture stirring constantly until the mixture becomes thick. Total cooking time is about 10 minutes. Do not use an aluminum bowl; it will cause the lemon curd to discolor.
This method of cooking the custard is called the double boiler method. (I recommend this method for the best results)
3. Remove from heat and Strain immediately.
4. Cut butter into small pieces and whisk into the mixture until butter has melted. As the mixture cools it will thicken further. Cover and use as needed.

*Curd will keep for weeks stored covered in the refrigerator.*
*Lemon curd makes an excellent flavoring or filling. It can also be used as a sauce by thinning with lemon juice or simple syrup.*

# Lemony Bread Pudding

*Makes two 9x13 baking pans*

### Ingredients
1 cup Butter
1 ½ quarts Heavy Cream
2 cans Sweetened Condensed Milk
Zest from two lemons finely diced
¼ cup fresh lemon juice
1 Tablespoon vanilla extract
½ cup light brown sugar
1 Tablespoon ground ginger
2 teaspoons cinnamon
3 ½ quarts Toasted bread crumbs
6 eggs

### Method
1. Crumble bread place on a baking sheet and toast until golden in color.
2. In a 4 quart sauce pan add butter and Heavy Cream. Put on medium heat to melt butter stirring constantly. Do not boil. When the Butter has melted, add sweet milk, sugar, lemon zest, vanilla and spices.
3. Slowly stir in bread crumbs. Mix well. Stir in eggs and lemon juice. Mix all together well.
4. Grease baking pans, Spoon bread pudding mixture into the pans.
5. Bake at 350º for 30 minutes.  Serve warm. Top with lemon curd or sweet potato syrup.

# *Angel Cake*
*Makes one 10 inch tube cake*

*This cake is very high and moist. The egg whites should be 70º.*
*Pre-heat oven to 350º. Have a 10-inch ready clean and ungreased.*

## *Ingredients*
1 cup cake flour sifted
¾ cup fine sugar
½ teaspoon salt
Sift the flour, sugar, and salt together 3 times. Reserve in a separate bowl.
Combine the following ingredients in a large bowl and beat on low speed for 1 minute:
1 ½ cups egg white
1 tablespoon water
1 tablespoon fresh lemon juice
1 teaspoon cream of tartar
1 teaspoon vanilla or other flavoring

## *Method*
1. On medium-high speed beat until the mixture increases 4 to 5 times in volume and looks like a bowl of foam. 3 to 5 minutes.
2. on medium-high speed. Beat in 1 tablespoon at a time ¾ **cup of sugar. 2 to 3 minutes.**
When all of the sugar is added, the foam will be creamy white and hold soft, moist, glossy peaks that bend over at the points. Do not beat until stiff.
3. Transfer the batter to a large wide bowl (4 to 6 quarts). **This will make folding easier.**
4. Sift a light layer of the flour over the batter evenly. Fold gently with a rubber spatula until the flour is incorporated. Only fold do not mix or stir.
5. Repeat the same process until flour is all incorporated.
6. Pour batter into pan. Level off the batter.
7. Bake at 350º, until when a toothpick is inserted into the center, comes out clean. 35 to 40 min.
8. Invert cake to cool. Once cooled, slide a thin knife around the cake to detach it from the pan. Do the same to the bottom of the cake. Cool cake completely before frosting or serve with fresh fruit. The blue berries from the blueberry key-lime pie works well with this cake. Yum Yum gimme some!!

# *Did Some One Say Pound Cake?*

The True Pound Cake is made with equal weights of the main ingredients, which was based on the weight of the eggs used in the mixture. It originated centuries ago and was highly spiced, flavored and perfumed with aromatic herbs. Pound cakes were also filled with seeds or dried fruit. For some the traditional recipe maybe considered to be a bit dry or even a bit heavy for today's tastes. Here is a recipe for Pound Cake that captures the rich and buttery flavor and texture of the True Pound Cake.

## *Light, Rich and Buttery Pound Cake*

*Have all ingredients at room temperature 70°. Pre-heat oven to 325° Grease and flour one 9x5 inch loaf pan.*

### *Ingredients*
2 cups cake flour sifted twice
5 medium eggs
2 sticks of unsalted butter
1 1/3 cups of sugar
¼ teaspoon salt
1 tablespoon vanilla extract

### *Method:*
1. In a medium bowl beat 5 eggs.
2. In a separate large mixing bowl add butter. Beat for 1 minute until creamy.
3. Gradually mix in sugar, salt and butter, beat for 5 minutes until creamy.
4. To the butter and sugar mixture, slowly add flour 1 cup at a time alternating with some egg. Mix well after each addition. Repeat until flour and eggs are fully incorporated into the batter. Be sure to scrape the sides of the bowl after each addition
5. Pour the batter into the pan and bake for about 1 hour and 10 minutes, or until a toothpick inserted comes out clean. Allow cake to cool, remove from the pan and serve.
 This is excellent served with fresh fruit and whipped cream.

# Classic Pound cake
## Hand-whipped

*Ingredients*
Step 1
1 pound butter (room temperature 70°)
3 cups sugar
2 tablespoons vanilla extract
6 large eggs
Step 1

*Method*
In a large bowl:
1. Whip together butter, vanilla and sugar. 5 min
2. Now add eggs one by one. Whip mixture for one minute after each egg is added until creamy and Fluffy.

Step 2
4 cups flour
2 tablespoons baking powder
¼ teaspoon salt
Mix dry ingredients and sift 4 times.

Step 3
Fold flour mixture into butter mixture 1 cup at a time. Incorporate well after each addition.
Mix in 1 cup heavy cream.
Step 4 pre-heat oven to 350°
Pour mixture into buttered floured pans.
One 10 inch bundt pan and two 9x5 loaf pans bake 1 hour to 1 hour 15 minutes

# *Spiced Rum Pound Cake*
(Have all ingredients room temp 70º)

*Step1*
**Ingredients**
1 cup butter
3 cups sugar
¼ cup rum
6 large eggs
1 cup sour cream

**Method**
1. Cream butter and sugar together until light and fluffy.
2. Add eggs, one at a time, beat well after each addition
3. Mix in rum
4. Mix in sour cream all at once.
*Step 2*
3 cups all-purpose flour
¼ teaspoon baking soda
1 teaspoon ground ginger
½ teaspoon cinnamon

**Method**
1. Sift flour together with other dry ingredients
2. Add dry ingredients to batter. Blend well
3. Pour batter into a well-greased and floured bundt or tube pan.
4. Bake at 325º for 1 to 1 ¼ hours.
5. Remove from oven. Allow To cool and remove from pan.
Ice the pound cake if you desire.

**Simple Rum Icing**
½ cup butter
1 box, 10x powdered sugar.
1 egg white
Rum for flavor (you decide the amount to add) start with 2 tablespoons Rum.
**Method**
1. Whip all ingredients together until well blended and creamy.
2. Add Rum icing to cooled cake.

# *Blueberry Dumplings*

**4 to 6 servings**
***Blueberry sauce***
*Step 1*
1 quart blueberries, rinsed
1 cup water
1cup sugar

***Method***
1. Mix blueberries with the water and sugar
2. Bring mixture to a boil in a 4 quart sauce pan.
3. Reduce heat and simmer for 5 minutes.

***Dumplin***
*Step 2*
11/2 cups flour
2 teaspoons baking powder
1 tablespoon sugar
¼ teaspoons salt
¼ teaspoon ginger
¼ teaspoon cinnamon
1/8 teaspoon nutmeg
2/3 cup (milk, water, or vanilla yogurt)

***Method***
In a medium size bowl:
1. Combine flour, sugar, baking powder, salt and spices. Mix well to disperse ingredients.
2. Add liquid and stir until mixed.
3. Drop by tablespoons into the simmering berry mixture.
4. Cover with a tight fitting lid and simmer 15 minutes.
Serve in bowls with a dollop of whipped cream or a scoop vanilla bean ice cream.

# Heirloom Blend Bean Salad

*Serve cold.*

*Ingredients*
8 oz packet of Heirloom Bean Blend (or other bean blend)
1 quart of water

*Step 1*
 Sort and pick over beans to remove any unwanted material.
Bring 1 quart of water to a boil in a medium size sauce pan. Remove from heat.
Add beans and soak for one hour. Drain beans.

*Step 2*
Prepare a spicy vegetable broth to cook bean blend in.
1 quart of water
½ tsp Dried Diced Chipotle peppers
½ tsp Granulated Garlic
¼ tsp Dry Thyme
½ tsp Herbs de Provence
½ tsp Dry Ground Ginger
¼ tsp Black Pepper
Season broth with salt or vegetable base to your taste
Add bean blend, bring mixture to a boil and cook until beans are tender.
Drain and cool.

*Step 3*
Compose salad in a large bowl. Add the following ingredients to beans.
4oz Extra Virgin Olive Oil
4 medium Vine-ripe Tomatoes (medium to large dice)
2 cups shredded carrots
1 cup celery diced small
½ cup green peppers medium dice
½ cup red pepper medium dice
½ to 1 cup pecan halves or pieces
¼ cup balsamic vinegar
Blend all ingredients well. Serve as a salad or a cold side dish.

# Stewed Organic Chicken Thighs with Baby Bella's

*Serves 5*

## Ingredients
1 ½ pounds free- range chicken thighs
Salt, pepper, granulated garlic, thyme, ground ginger, all-purpose flour
½ cup vegetable oil

## Method
1. Season chicken with salt, pepper, garlic, thyme and ginger.
2. Dredge chicken in flour. Shake off excess flour.
3. In a large sauté pan, over medium heat, pour in vegetable oil.
4. Allow oil to get hot but not smoking hot.
5. Add chicken thighs, brown on both sides. Remove from pan and reserve until later.

## Step2
## Ingredients (All small diced)
¼ cup onions
¼ cup celery
¼ cup green peppers
¼ cup red peppers
1 cup sliced baby Porto Bella's
¼ cup vegetable oil
12 oz rich chicken or vegetable broth

## Method
1. In a 4 quart sauce pan, add oil and all vegetables.
2. Lightly season vegetables with salt, pepper, garlic and herbs.
3. Sauté until the vegetables are tender then dust with 3 tablespoons of all-purpose flour.
4. Stir until well incorporated.
5. Stir in chicken broth. Add chicken thighs, cover with a tight fitting lid.
6. Simmer for 45 min. serve hot.

# *Herb Roasted Potato Medley*

Serves 8 to 12

## *Ingredients*
3 medium red skin or new potatoes
3 medium purple potatoes
3 medium Yukon Gold potatoes
1 jumbo sweet potato
1 medium onion sliced
Step1: Use unblemished potatoes for best results

## *Method*
1. Wash and scrub potatoes (peel if needed)
2. Medium dice all potatoes.
3. Place potatoes in a large bowl with sliced onion
4. To bowl add ½ cup olive oil.
5. Season potatoes with salt, black pepper, granulated garlic, thyme and Herbs of Provence.
6. Toss potatoes and onion coating well with the oil and herbs.

## *Step2*
1. Pre-heat oven to 350°.
2. Pour potatoes into a baking dish cover dish with a tight fitting lid or foil.
3. Bake for 30 to 45 minutes or until potatoes are fork tender. Serve hot. ENJOY!

# *Vegetable Broth Lamb Stew*

Serves 8

## *Ingredients*
2 lbs Lamb Stew Meat medium cubed
1 medium red onion diced
2 medium organic carrots roll cut
3 ribs celery medium sliced
2 cups diced potato blend (2 red potatoes, 2 Yukon Gold potatoes, 2 purple potatoes, 1 small sweet potato)
scrub potatoes well, peel if skin is not desired.
1 tablespoon chopped garlic
1 tablespoon herbs of Provence
1 teaspoon thyme leaves
¼ cup olive oil
4 cups vegetable broth
1 big tablespoon of vegetable base paste
Salt and Pepper
4 quart stock pot

## *Method:*
1. Season Lamb with salt and pepper.
2. Brown the meat in a large sauce pan. 3 minutes on high heat.
3. Add onion, carrots and celery. Sauté on medium heat for 5 minutes.
4. Add garlic and herbs. Stir. Add potatoes and sauté for 5 minutes.
5. Add broth, bring to a boil and then reduce to a simmer. Add vegetable base, stir to incorporate.
6. Allow meat to simmer until tender stirring occasionally. About 45 minutes.
7. If needed add more salt or other seasonings to taste.

# *ROUX*

*Roux is the most common thickener for savory sauces. The mixture is composed of a fat and flour, usually in equal amounts. The fat smoothes out the flour so as not to clump when mixed with a liquid.*

*A Roux is made by melting or heating the fat, adding flour and cooking over low heat while whisking or stirring constantly. Important to cook slow cooking fast makes it grainy and unusable.*

This recipe yields 1 quart of roux.

### Ingredients
1 pound clarified butter or oil
1 pound flour

### Method
1. Heat the clarified butter or oil in a medium thick bottom sauce pan (3 quart) over medium heat.
2. Add the flour all at once. Stir constantly, cook over low heat until the roux is pale ivory and has a nutty aroma. 3 to 5 minutes. Roux should be glossy in appearance.
3. If the roux will not be used right away, cool and store it tightly wrapped in the refrigerator.
4. 1 tablespoon of roux will thicken 1 cup of liquid

## *The application of* combining white roux with liquid
1. Be sure that the roux and liquid temperatures are different. Hot liquid is added to cold roux. Hot roux is added to cold liquid. This helps prevent lumping. Add one to the other slowly and whip to work out lumps.
2. Gradually return soup or sauce to a boil whisking constantly.
3. Reduce heat while stirring and simmer for 20 min to cook out the flour taste (starch)
4. To test for doneness, taste sauce between the roof of the mouth and tongue. If it steel feels gritty or tastes gluey continue cooking until the starch is cooked out.

# *Béchamel*

*This is a basic white sauce (Mother Sauce) known by chefs for its neutral flavor character and smooth texture. Its uses include creaming foods like vegetables and fish, and as a base to make other sauces and cream soups. (Uses: she-crab soup, butternut and shrimp bisque and macaroni and cheese)*
Yield: two quarts

### *Ingredients:*
2 ½ quarts Milk
8 ounces White Roux (room temp) to make thicker add 4 oz more roux.
Salt to taste ½ teaspoon
White pepper to taste ¼ teaspoon

*Method*: prepare sauce in a heavy bottom 3 quart sauce pan
1. Scald the milk (do not boil) **Scald** means to heat a liquid, usually a dairy product, in a saucepan until it almost boils. You will know that it is scalded when a film forms on the surface of the milk.
2. Pour it over the roux while constantly whisking and slowly bringing the mixture to a boil.
3. Simmer for 30 minutes.
4. Season to taste
5. If sauce is too lumpy, strain through a strainer or a doubled cheese cloth.

*Make sauce a little thicker than you think it should be. It is easier to thin out a sauce than to thicken it.*
*For creamed dished use 1 cup of cream to 2 cups of solids.*
*Be sure to save final seasonings until you taste the mixture.*
*Béchamel sauce can be refrigerated or kept warm in the top of a double boiler for up to an hour.*
*To avoid a skin from forming on top of the sauce, place wax paper or plastic wrap directly on the surface of the sauce.*

# Rich Vegetable Stock

*The goal of making a vegetable stock is to draw all of the flavor profile out of the vegetables. Stock can be made with a variety of vegetables. Vegetable stock may be used for vegetarian-style soups, stews, bean dishes and rice.*

## Ingredients
2 carrots, peeled and diced
2 parsnips, peeled and diced
2 leeks cut in half and wash each layer well to remove all grit and then slice
1 large onion, diced
2 cups celery diced with leaves
8 oz mushrooms with stems, sliced (use a mixture, button and wild)
8 cloves of garlic smash them then peel (not 8 heads, but cloves)
6 sprigs of parsley
2 tbsp herbs of Provence
1 tbsp thyme
1 tbsp sage
4 tbsp cold pressed extra virgin olive oil

## Method
1. Heat olive oil in a 4 quart stock pot over medium-high heat.
2. Add and cook all vegetables stirring occasionally, until well browned (caramelized).
3. Cover the vegetables with cold water. Add the parsley and other herbs.
4. Simmer gently, uncovered, until the vegetables are very tender, 45 to 60 minutes. Skim any impurities from the stock. Strain, press down on vegetables to extract all juice. Allow to cool uncovered. When cool cover and then refrigerate. Use as needed.

# LOW COUNTRY FAVORITES

## Savory Collard Greens
*Greens are a healthy part of any diet.*
*These greens are very easy to prepare.*

### Ingredients
2 large bunches of Collards Greens
1 cup chopped yellow onions
1 cup sliced or medium diced celery
1 large turnip root medium dice 2 cups
2 medium sized parsnips diced 1 to 2 cups
1 cup shredded carrots
¼ cup chopped garlic
½ cup butter (or vegetable spread, vegetable oil, or olive oil)
3 tablespoons Herbs of Provence
1 tablespoon thyme
1 tablespoon oregano
2 tablespoons ground ginger
1 tablespoon cumin
1 tablespoon chili powder
½ cup brown sugar packed
1 cup Balsamic vinegar
½ cup vegetable base paste
1 gallon water

### Method
1. Thoroughly wash greens to remove all dirt and unwanted debris
2. Strip greens from the stem and roughly chop. Hold in a large bowl.
3. In a 4 quart stock pot add butter, onions, celery, carrots, parsnips, garlic and turnips. Over medium-high heat, sauté for 5 minutes.
4. Add all spices to mixture, stir to incorporate.
5. Pour in water, sugar, vegetable paste and balsamic vinegar. Bring to a boil. Taste broth, if needed add salt to season to your taste.
6. Add Collards. Boil 45 minutes to 1 hour until tender.

# Low Country Red Rice

*This is my version of Low Country Red Rice. This red rice dish is seasoned to perfection and made with no meat. This rice is made Vegan Style. This rice goes well with Collard greens, fish and any bean dish.*

## Ingredients
1/3 cup vegetable oil, butter or margarine
½ cup diced red onion small or medium diced
1/3 cup diced red bell peppers
1/3 cup diced green bell peppers
½ cup shredded carrots
½ cup diced celery
2 tbsp chopped garlic
1 tsp cumin
1 tsp chili powder
2 tbsp sugar
2 tsp herbs of Provence
2 tsp black pepper
1 tsp thyme
1 tsp oregano
2 tsp ground ginger
1 cup diced tomatoes
1 cup crushed tomatoes
2 cups water
 2 cups parboiled long grain white rice
¼ to ½ cup vegetable base paste or salt to taste

## Method
1. In a 3 quart sauce pan, add vegetable oil over medium high heat
2. Add onions, carrots, celery, peppers and garlic. Sauté vegetables 5 minutes.
3. Add black pepper, and other spice. Add tomato and simmer 5 min.
4. Add water, bring to a boil. Season the tomato broth with vegetable paste or salt to taste. Do not over season your broth.
5. Add rice. Bring to a boil, and then reduce to a simmer while stirring occasionally. This rice will stick and burn on the bottom if not carefully attended. Simmer rice for 25 to 30 minutes or until rice is tender.

# Stewed Tomatoes and Okra

*Serves 8*

### Ingredients
1/3 cup vegetable oil, butter, or margarine
½ cup diced red onion small or medium diced
1/2 cup diced red bell peppers
1/2 cup diced green bell peppers
½ cup shredded carrots
½ cup diced celery
2 tbsp chopped garlic
1 tbsp herbs of Provence
1 tsp black pepper
1 tsp thyme
1 tsp oregano
2 tsp ground ginger
2 cups diced tomatoes
2 cups crushed tomatoes
2 tsp basil
1 cup water
5 cups frozen or fresh sliced okra
¼ cup vegetable base paste or salt to taste

### Method
1. In a 3 quart sauce pan, add vegetable oil, over medium high heat
2. Add onions, carrots, celery, peppers and garlic. Sauté 5 minutes.
3. Add black pepper, and other spices. Add tomato and simmer 5 min.
4. Add water, bring to a boil. Season the tomato broth with vegetable paste or salt to taste. Do not over season your broth.
5. Add Okra. Bring to a boil, and then reduce to a simmer while stirring. Simmer okra and tomato for 15 to 20 minutes or until okra is tender.
*This dish can be served as a side, or over any of the rice recipes in this book.*

# Low Country Shrimp Gumbo

*Makes 1 ½ Quarts*

## Ingredients
1 lb 21/25 count jumbo shrimp peeled (de-vein if desired)
¼ cup vegetable oil
½ cup chopped red onions
½ cup medium diced green, bell peppers
½ cup medium diced red, bell peppers
½ cup celery, sliced
1 tsp chopped garlic
1 tsp black pepper
2 tbsp old bay
1 tbsp lobster or shrimp base
1 tsp ginger
1 tsp herbs of Provence
1 tsp thyme
3 to 4 cups sliced okra
2 to 3 cups diced tomato
1 to 2 cups water

## Method
1. In a 3 quart sauce pan, heat vegetable oil over medium high heat.
2. Add onion, bell peppers, celery and garlic. Sauté 3 minutes. Add black pepper and other herbs. Cook 2 minutes, then add shrimp. Sauté 5 minutes.
3. Add the okra, Sauté 5 minutes. Add diced tomato. Bring to a simmer, then season to taste with salt or seafood base. Cook 15 to 20 minutes until done.
*Try some rice or grits with your gumbo. Nothing could be finer.*

# White Rice

*12 Servings*    This Recipe uses parboiled rice
## Ingredients
5 cups long grain rice
4 ½ cups water
2 teaspoons Herbs of Provence
2 teaspoons parsley
Salt to taste
2 tablespoons butter

## Method
1. Rinse and drain rice.
2. Pour water into a four quart. sauce pan add spices, salt and butter. Bring to a boil.
3. Add rice and stir. Return to a boil. Stir.
4. Reduce Heat and cook for 30 minutes or until water is absorbed.
5. Reduce heat to low and simmer allowing rice to steam for 15 minutes. When rice is tender it is ready to serve.
**NOTE: The rice goes well with the collard greens and the chicken recipe featured earlier.**

# Brown Rice

Serves 12
## Ingredients
3 cups Brown rice
5 cups water
2 tablespoons butter
1 tablespoon Herbs of Provence
Season to taste with salt or vegetable base paste

## Method
1. Rinse and drain rice.
2. Pour water into a four quart sauce pan add spices, salt and butter. Bring to a boil.
3. Add rice and stir. Return to a boil. Stir.
4. Reduce Heat and cook for 30 minutes or until water is absorbed.
5. Reduce heat to low and simmer allowing rice to steam for 15 minutes. When rice is tender it is ready to serve.
*NOTE: The rice goes especially well with the collard greens, stewed lamb and the chicken recipe featured earlier.*

# Low Country Grits (Gullah Style)

4 cups water
½ cup butter
1 cup Old fashioned (stone ground grits)
½ teaspoon black pepper
1/2 teaspoon Garlic
Optional * ½ teaspoon herbs of Provence

## Method

1. In a 3 quart sauce pan, bring water, butter and seasonings to a boil.
2. Stir in grits. Cook stirring for 10 minutes on low-medium heat.
3. Reduce heat to a low simmer and cook for 20 minutes more while stirring. The grits should look creamy; if they are too thick add more water or milk if desired. Season grits with salt to taste, at the end of cooking if desired. If you season too early in the cooking process, as the liquid evaporates the salt or seasoning will intensify and may become salty.
4. When done serve them with everything you like. Grits taste good and they are a versatile side dish.
Notes: serve with sautéed shrimp and onions with fresh tomatoes and basil. Serve with gumbo, bean dishes, scrambled eggs, Fresh vegetables or you can even make grits cakes. It's like polenta but its grits.

# Low Country Mac-n-Cheese
## Gullah Style

### Ingredients

2 large eggs (lightly scrambled)
½ cup butter
1 cup of milk or heavy cream (Béchamel can be used)
8 oz or more of sharp cheddar cheese shredded 4 oz cubed
1 tablespoon salt
1 tablespoon of black pepper
1 box Elbow Macaroni Noodles
4 cups of water to boil noodles

### Method:

1. Pre-heat oven to 350º
2. Boil macaroni noodles with salt and water until tender. Box instructions are accurate.
3. When macaroni is done, drain off water and reserve the noodles in a large bowl.
4. Blend in the other ingredients.  Pour into a casserole dish.
5. Bake for 20 to 30 minutes or until done. Until lightly brown on top.
Serve warm.

# Sun-Dried Tomato and Lentil Soup

*6 servings*

## Ingredients
2 cups julienne Sun dried tomato store bought
1 ½ cups dried lentils
3 tablespoons olive oil
1 medium yellow onion, minced
1 medium carrot peeled, minced or shredded
2 ribs of celery, minced
6 cups of rich vegetable stock
1 pound new red potatoes, washed and quartered
1 tablespoon fresh rosemary, minced
2 teaspoons herb of Provence
1 tablespoon garlic, minced
Kosher salt and freshly ground black pepper, season to taste

## Method
1. Pick over lentil to remove unwanted debris. Wash lentils. Place in a bowl of hot water for 1 hour or over night. Drain and set aside.
2. In a 4 quart sauce pan over medium heat, add oil, onions celery and carrots. Sauté for 2 minutes then add garlic and herbs of Provence. Sauté 2 minutes more. The veggies should be light brown.
3. Add the stock, lentils, potatoes and tomatoes. Bring to a boil. Reduce heat and simmer with no cover. Cook until potatoes and lentils are tender 30 to 40 minutes.
4. Add the rosemary and continue to simmer. Stir gently and simmer 15 minutes.
5. Season with salt and pepper to taste. Serve hot!

# Butternut Squash & Shrimp Bisque

*Serves 12*

**Ingredients**

3 each Butternut Squash, peeled and diced

1 pound 71/90 ct. shrimp peeled and de-veined

1 cup Butter

1 medium onion, Diced small

½ cup carrots peeled and shredded

¼ cup each green peppers and red peppers

½ cup seafood base

¼ cup minced garlic

4 cups heavy cream or Béchamel sauce

¼ cup chopped parsley (fresh)

1tsp dry thyme

1 tablespoon Herbs of Provence

To your taste, carefully season with salt and pepper

**Method**

1. In a 4 quart heavy sauce pan. Melt butter over medium heat.

2. Add the squash and garlic. Cook for 5 to 10 minutes. Stir mixture constantly.

3. Add the onions, carrots and peppers.

4. Sauté until the mixture looks like mush. Add the seafood base and shrimp. Cook for 5 minutes. Add thyme and herbs of Provence.

5. Add Cream, 1 cup at a time, Stir to incorporate cream.

6. Bring to a simmer and cook for 10 minutes. Add parsley.

7. Season to taste with salt and white pepper.

*Note: If the soup consistency is too thick add more cream or milk.*

# Hilton Head She-Crab Soup

*About 12 cups*

*Step 1*
1 pound, cleaned crab roe
If your crab roe is not cleaned add 8 ounces of water to your crab roe, 4 bay leafs, 4 ounces of white wine, 2 tablespoons of old bay.
Bring this mixture to a boil. Remove from heat and strain the roe to separate from bone and bay leaf. Reserve the mixture. Discard bones.

*Step 2*
Over low heat in a large 4 qt sauce pan melt butter.
4 tablespoons butter
Add ¼ cup of the following finely diced (shallot, green pepper, red pepper, celery, carrots)
Lightly sauté or sweat these ingredients. 2 minutes
Whisk in:
4 tablespoons all-purpose flour
Continue to whisk flour and cook it until the mixture smells nutty but not brown. About 3 minutes.
Remove the pan from the heat and slowly whisk in 5 cups of milk.
Bring this mixture back to the stove over medium heat, bringing it to a simmer. Continue to whisk until thickened and looks smooth. Reduce heat.

*Step 3*
Stir in the following ingredients.
Crab roe
1 pound of crab meat cleaned of shells
½ cup of dry sherry
Kosher salt and pepper to taste
1 teaspoon thyme leaf
1 teaspoon herbs of Provence
Heat mixture gently to warm crab meat to 145°. Serve and enjoy!

# *Jerk Marinade*

Makes 2 ½ quarts

### *Ingredients*
1/3 cup fresh squeezed lemon juice
1 ½ cups packed light brown sugar
1 ½ cups orange juice concentrate
1 cup Nelly & Joe's Key West Key-lime Juice
¼ cup Jamaican Jerk Seasoning
¼ cup dry parsley
1 tablespoon dry thyme
4 teaspoons table grind black pepper
1 quart teriyaki sauce
¼ cup chopped garlic
2 cups vegetable oil

### *Method*
1. Put all ingredients in a large bowl and mix well.
2. This marinade can be used on any meat, poultry, seafood and vegetables.
Marinate for 1 hour to overnight. Bake, Grill, or sauté as you wish.
This marinade can also be used as a salad dressing.

# Shrimp Burger

*Makes 12 8oz burgers*

## Ingredients
5 pounds 71/90 count shrimp (fresh or frozen)
½ cup red onions chopped fine (squeeze out excess liquid)
¼ cup green bell peppers chopped fine (squeeze out excess liquid)
¼ cup red bell peppers chopped fine (squeeze out excess liquid)
½ cup celery chopped fine (squeeze out excess liquid)
1 to 2 tablespoons chopped garlic
1 tablespoon table grind black pepper
1 tablespoon dry thyme
½ cup dry parsley
6 ounces salad oil
4 to 6 tablespoons Old Bay Seasoning

## Method
1. If frozen, thaw shrimp. Then drain of excess water.
2. Remove 1 pound of shrimp and place into a large mixing bowl.
3. In a food processor chop ½ of the remaining shrimp to a medium consistency. Remove and place into bowl with whole shrimp.
4. Put the remaining shrimp into the food processor and chop into a fine consistency. Remove and add to bowl.
5. Add all remaining ingredients and mix well with a rubber spatula. Add salt to taste. Store shrimp burger in refrigerator.
6. To cook Shrimp Burgers, use a large ice cream scoop to portion burgers about 6 to 8 ounces. Cook burgers on a flat top grill or in a large sauté pan.
7. Cook on medium-high heat for 2 ½ minutes per side until done.
8. Serve on a Kaiser roll with the condiments of your choice.
Good companions include: (cocktail sauce, cheddar cheese, lettuce, tomato, grilled onions, avocados, etc…

# Baking or Roasting Fish

*I highly recommend this way of cooking fish. Fish is very delicate when cooked, this method of cookery helps to preserve the integrity of the fish helping it to remain intact and retain its subtle flavor.*

# Slow roasted Salmon or Tilapia

*This gentle method of cooking fish guarantees that the fish remains moist and tender*

*4 servings*

### Ingredients
1 ½ to 2 lbs skinned fish filets, rinse and pat dry
Olive oil or butter
Salt, pepper, granulated garlic
Herbs of Provence
1 lemon
4 oz white wine (optional)

### Method
Pre-heat oven to 325°
1. Spray a baking dish or a half sheet pan with pan coating or use olive oil sparingly.
2. Rub fish with olive oil or butter
3. Season with salt, pepper and garlic to taste. Lightly sprinkle with herbs of Provence. Lay fish in roasting pan. Squeeze lemon juice over fish then wine.
4. Place fish in oven. Roast undisturbed, after 15 minutes of baking, check the internal temperature of the fish. When the temperature reaches 125° to 130° remove the fish from the oven, allow the fish to stand for 3 minutes and then serve. You can also check for doneness by flaking a bit of the fish off. If it is opaque throughout, it is done.
** garnish with lemons and minced parsley**
*** Good accompaniments include, baked sweet potatoes, rice, grits or over a bed of mixed greens***
Enjoy!!!

# Sweet Potato Cornbread™

*This is the original recipe for Chef David Vincent Young's Sweet Potato Cornbread™ served at The Sea Shack, on Hilton Head Island, SC. Whenever I make Sweet Potato Cornbread; this is the batch size that I make. If you want to bake for a large group this recipe is great, however; there is a smaller version in the front of this book.*

*It took over a year to perfect this recipe. It is easier for me to make something just from feeling and tasting, rather than harnessing a flavor with words to put it on paper. I had to test many different formulations and ingredients to find the perfect union of flavor and spice. After many taste tests, here it is. I wrote it just for you.*

*Dchef's Sweet Potato Cornbread*

*Serves 80*
*Makes 4: 12x13x2 rectangular baking pans or 2 hotel pans*

### Part 1:

This recipe starts with cooking the sweet potatoes in simple syrup. This is also the beginning process for making candied yams (sweet potatoes). The process of cooking the sweet potatoes in the simple syrup really intensifies the flavor of the sweet potato.

**Step1: Boil the sweet potato and make sweet potato syrup.**
1. Scrub and peel 12 medium sweet potatoes.
2. Cut potatoes into medium diced pieces. Place in a 4 quart sauce pan.
3. Add 4 cups of sugar and 2 cups of light brown sugar packed. Cover with water.
4. Boil until tender, 25 to 35 minutes. Test for doneness with a fork
5. Drain, and reserve the sweet potato simple syrup. Bring the simple syrup back to a boil. Boil until syrup thickens. Allow to cool. Reserve the syrup for other uses. This syrup is used as a glaze to top the sweet potato cornbread when it comes out of the oven.
6. Hold the sweet potatoes in a large bowl or baking pan.

**Step2: Sweet potato cornbread batter**
### Ingredients
4 cups fine cornmeal
3 cups medium to coarse cornmeal
5 cups all-purpose flour
2 cups white sugar
1 pound light brown sugar
¾ cup baking powder

½ cup ground ginger

1/8 cup to ¼ cup Jamaican Jerk seasoning

3 tablespoons cinnamon

4 cups sour dressing (imitation sour cream) or sour cream

2 cups liquid margarine or melted butter flavored shortening

1 cup vanilla extract

4 to 5 cups Water (use as needed) if the mixture is too dry use more water.

8 cups boiled sweet potatoes from **step1** above. (Do not pack in cup)

*Method*

1. In a large mixing bowl, combine all dry ingredients, mix well to incorporate all ingredients.

2. Make a well in the center of mixture.

3. Add vanilla, shortening, sour cream, and 4 cups of sweet potatoes.

4. Mix with a rubber spatula from the center. Add 1 cup of water at a time. Mix well. The batter should be soft but not runny.

5. Fold in remaining sweet potatoes.

6. Moderately grease baking pans. Fill each pan about ¾ full.

7. Bake in a 350° oven for 60 to 90 min. Check for doneness by inserting a knife or toothpick. When inserted and comes out clean, cornbread is done.

8. Remove from oven and drizzle with sweet potato syrup. Cool for 30 minutes then serve.

# COMMON BAKING EQUIVALENTS and INGREDIENT MEASUREMENTS

**Baking Powder**
1 ounce = 2 tablespoons
¼ ounce = 1 ½ teaspoons
1 teaspoon = 0.17 ounces
1 tablespoon = 0.5 ounces
1 cup = 8 ounces

**Cocoa, Unsifted**
1 ounce = 5 tablespoons
1 cup = 3.2 ounces
1 pound = 5 cups
1 tablespoon = .2 ounce

**Cream of Tartar**
1 ounce = 4 tablespoons
¼ ounce = 1 tablespoon
1 teaspoon = .08 ounce
1 cup = 6 ounces

**Salt**
1 ounce = 5 teaspoons
¼ ounce = 1 ¼ teaspoons
1 teaspoon = .2 ounce
1 cup = 10 ounces

**Cinnamon**
1 ounce = 5 tablespoons plus 2 teaspoons
¼ ounce= 4 ¼ teaspoons
1 teaspoon = .06 ounces
1 tablespoon = .31 ounces
1 cup = 5 ounces

**Cocoa, Unsifted**
1 tablespoon = .2 ounce
1 ounce = 5 tablespoons
1 cup = 3.2 ounces
1 pound = 5 cups

**Cornstarch, Unsifted**
1 tablespoon = .25 ounce
1 ounce = 3 ½ tablespoons
1 cup = 4.5 ounces
1 pound = 3 ½ cups

**Confectioners' Sugar, Sifted**
1 cup = 4 ounces
1 pound = 4 cups

**Confectioners' Sugar, Unsifted**
1 cup = 4.5 ounces
1 pound = 3 ½ cups

**Granulated, Sugar**
1 cup = 7 ounces
1 pound = 2 ¼ cups

**Brown, Sugar**
1 cup = 5.25 ounces
1 pound = 2 ½ cups packed

**Ground Spices, (except cinnamon)**
1 ounce = 4 tablespoons plus 2 teaspoons
¼ ounce = 3 ½ teaspoons
½ cup = 4 ounces

**All- Purpose Flour**
1 cup = 4 ounces
1 pound = 2 ½ cups packed

**Bread Flour, Unsifted**
1 cup = 4.75 ounces
1 pound = 4 cups

**Cake, Flour**
1 pound = 3 ¾ cups
1 cup = 3.75 ounces

**Cornmeal**
1 pound = 3 cups

**Grated Lemon Zest**

    1 ounce = 4 tablespoons

    1 teaspoon = .08 ounce

**Garlic**

    1 small clove = 1/8 teaspoon powdered

    ¼ teaspoon granulated

    ½ teaspoon minced

**Potatoes**

    1 pound or 3 medium sized potatoes =

    3 ½ to 4 cups raw potatoes sliced or diced

    2 ½ cups cooked, 1 ¾ cups mashed

**Rice**

    1 pound = 3 ½ cups = 6 cups cooked

**Grits**

    Follow guide on package!

**Butter**

    1 pound = 2 cups

    1 stick = 4 ounces

    1 stick = 8 tablespoons

**Fresh, Greens**

    1 pound = 10 cups chopped

**Mushrooms, Fresh**

    8 ounces or 3 cups whole =

    About 1 cup cooked = 1 ½ cups sliced

**Eggs, Whole**

    4 Jumbo or Extra-Large = about 1 cup

    5 Large or Medium = about 1 cup

    16 = about 1 quart

**Egg Whites**

    5 Jumbo = about 1 cup

    6 Extra-Large = about 1 cup

    7 Large = about 1 cup

**Egg Yolks**

    11 jumbo = 1 cup

    12 Extra-Large = about 1 cup

    14 Large = about 1 cup

**Pecans**

    1 pound shelled = about 4 ½ cups

**Turnips**

    1 pound = 2 ½ cups cubed

**Carrots, Parsnips**

    1 pound = 2 ½ cups sliced

**Onions, White, Red, Yellow**

    1 pound = 2 ½ cups chopped or sliced

**Celery**

    1 pound = 2 ½ cups chopped

    Bell Peppers, Fresh

    6 ounces or 1 large = 1 cup diced

**Okra**

    1 pound = 4 ½ cups sliced

**Water**

    16 ounces = 1 pint

    1pint=1pound

**Thank You all and I hope you get a copy of my next Cookbook**

**BURNIN' DOWN SOUTH II**
**Welcome to my Cookingdom**

**CONTACT**

**CHEF DAVID VINCENT YOUNG**

**dchef_1999@yahoo.com**

**To order Burnin' Down South™ Seasoning Salt, Hot Sauce, Herbs de Provence herb blend, To schedule a cooking class, for book signings or to ask any questions about recipe preparation.**

LaVergne, TN USA
22 March 2010
176766LV00002B